# Looking for Changes

by Margie O'Hern

Scott Foresman
is an imprint of

Glenview, Illinois • Boston, Massachusetts • Chandler, Arizona •
Upper Saddle River, New Jersey

**Illustrations**
**4, 14, 15** Jared Osterhold.

**Photographs**

Every effort has been made to secure permission and provide appropriate credit for photographic material. The publisher deeply regrets any omission and pledges to correct errors called to its attention in subsequent editions.

Unless otherwise acknowledged, all photographs are the property of Pearson Education, Inc.

**Cover** DEA Picture Library/Getty Images; **1** tbkmedia.de/Alamy Images; **3** NASA; **5** tbkmedia.de/Alamy Images; **6** Jupiter Images; **7** NASA; **8** United States Department of the Interior; **10** ©DK Images; **11** John Woodcock/©DK Images; **12** Jupiter Images; **13** Michael Dwyer/Alamy Images.

ISBN 13: 978-0-328-51649-0
ISBN 10:      0-328-51649-X

4 5 6 7 8 9 10 V0FL 15 14 13 12 11

# Changes on Earth

Did you know that Earth is changing all the time? Scientists study these changes to better understand them. They may, for example, study how a river changes course or how a lake dries up. Some of the most important changes today may be happening because of global warming. Global warming means that Earth is slowly getting warmer. A warmer Earth will change our weather and how living things on Earth survive.

Earth as seen from space

# The Arctic Ocean

One of the places scientists study is the Arctic Ocean. This ocean covers the northern part of Earth and contains the North Pole. In winter, the Arctic faces away from the Sun. During this time it is dark all day and all night. In summer, it faces the Sun. The result is that the Arctic is light all day and all night.

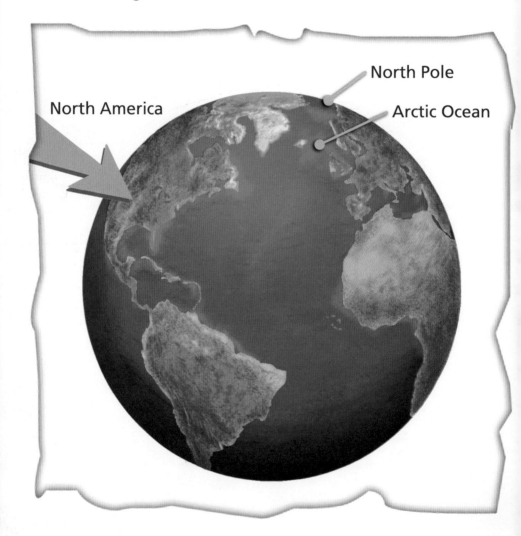

North Pole

North America

Arctic Ocean

Part of the Arctic Ocean is always covered by ice. The surface of the ocean can be -50°F in the winter. On the temperature **scale**, that's very, very cold. The ice can be 10 feet thick. **Pressure** ridges can be 30 feet thick. In winter, ice covers the entire ocean. In summer, pieces of ice float on the surface of the ocean.

Ice floating in the Arctic Ocean

The Arctic Ocean is surrounded by land that is frozen most of the year. Some small plants and some animals, such as polar bears, live on this land. Polar bears travel across the ice to hunt for the seals that live in the ocean. What will happen to the polar bears if there is no ice?

A polar bear in the Arctic

# Changes in the Arctic Ocean

Scientists study the Arctic Ocean. The **apprentices** who work with them drill holes in the ice. They measure the thickness of it. They study satellite pictures as well. They help the scientists write **essays** about what they are learning. From their work, we have learned the Arctic ice is melting a little bit more each year.

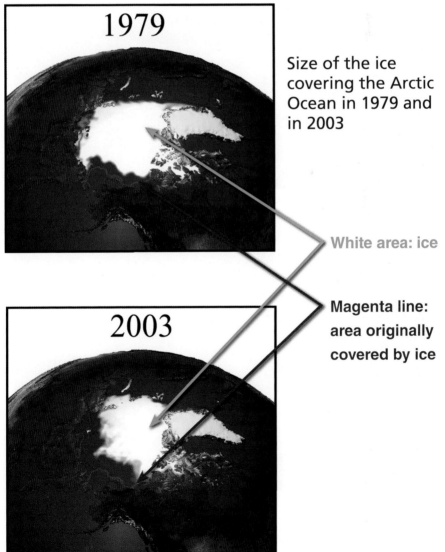

Size of the ice covering the Arctic Ocean in 1979 and in 2003

White area: ice

Magenta line: area originally covered by ice

A glacier is a river of ice. Scientists took pictures of a glacier 60 years ago. They also took pictures of the same glacier recently. The glacier is smaller now. Much of the ice in the glacier has melted. Warmer temperatures on Earth caused this melting.

Muir Glacier in August 1941

Muir Glacier in August 2004

# Global Warming

Global warming means Earth is getting warmer. Why do many scientists think this? They reviewed temperature records from 100 years ago. They wanted to see how warm it was then. Then, they checked the temperatures today. They discovered that Earth is warmer now. Many scientists think Earth may get even warmer in the future.

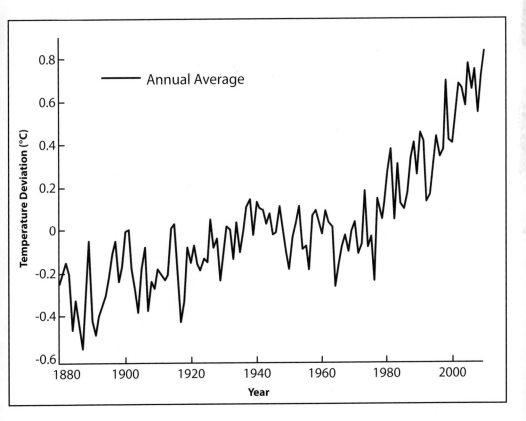

Average yearly temperature deviation from 0°C in the Northern Hemisphere

# Causes of Global Warming

Some scientists say that the greenhouse effect is making Earth warmer. Greenhouses are small glass buildings. People grow plants in them. The sunlight enters the greenhouse, but the Sun's heat can't get out. The air in the greenhouse stays warm. The plants inside grow well in the warm air.

A greenhouse

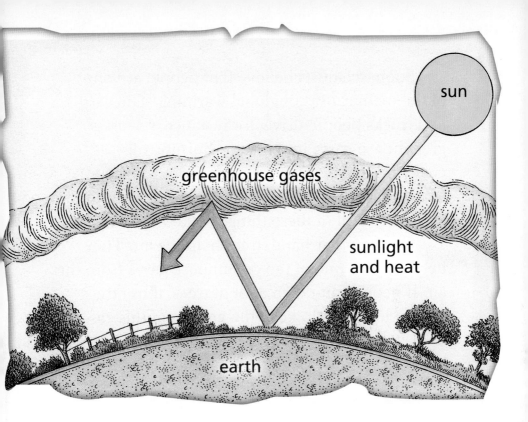

sun

greenhouse gases

sunlight and heat

earth

Earth's **atmosphere** can be like a greenhouse. Gases in the atmosphere hold in the warm air like the glass in the greenhouse. We call these gases greenhouse gases.

Many greenhouse gases occur naturally. We need *some* greenhouse gases. They let sunlight in and keep the Sun's heat on Earth. Living things need that warmth to stay alive.

However, today we have more greenhouse gases in our atmosphere than we used to. These gases keep more of the Sun's heat, so Earth is getting warmer and warmer. How might this have happened?

Some scientists believe that people are one of the main causes of global warming. The cars and trucks people drive, for instance, release greenhouse gases into the air. Burning oil, coal, and wood also adds these gases to the air. **Manufacturing** goods can put **chemicals** into the air as well. All of these things make Earth warmer.

On the other hand, trees help the air. They help remove one of the greenhouse gases from the air. If people cut down a lot of trees, those trees can no longer help keep the air free of this gas.

Some factories pollute Earth's atmosphere.

# Global Warming: Effects on Earth

In the future, it is possible that global warming could be responsible for more changes on Earth. For instance, ocean waters might rise. Coastal lands might become flooded and stay under water. The number of storms might increase, and they might become stronger.

Some places on Earth might get less rain. They might become hotter and drier. Inland lakes and rivers might shrink. Forest fires might increase. There might be less water to raise crops for food. Some plants and animals might disappear from Earth.

However, there is a lot we can all do to make sure that these changes don't happen.

A flooded area

# How to Help

You can help keep Earth from getting warmer. Here are some ideas:

Ride your bike or walk whenever you can. Suggest to your parents that your family leave the car home as much as possible. That way you won't be adding as many greenhouse gases to the air.

Turn off your computer when you're not using it. Turn off lights. Turn off the television. You will save electricity.

Recycle bottles, cans, plastic, glass, and paper. You will save energy and trees.

Talk to your parents about solar energy. Suggest that they think about heating your house with the Sun's energy.

Talk to your parents about cars. Suggest that they buy an energy-efficient car.

Learn as much as you can about the environment. Read books and talk to people. Start a **club** to help others learn more.

# Glossary

**apprentice** *n.* someone who works under a professional to learn an art or trade

**atmosphere** *n.* the mixture of gases that surrounds a planet

**chemical** *n.* a substance made by means of chemistry

**club** *n.* a group of people with a common interest

**essay** *n.* a short piece of written work

**manufacturing** *v.* to make something from raw materials

**pressure** *n.* the applying of force against something

**scales** *n.* systems of measurement